ENVIRONMENTAL, SOCIAL, AND GOVERNANCE ASSESSMENT OF MONGOLIA'S MINING SECTOR

MARCH 2026

ASIAN DEVELOPMENT BANK

ADB

6 ADB Avenue, Mandaluyong City, 1550 Metro Manila, Philippines
Tel +63 2 8632 4444; Fax +63 2 8636 2444
www.adb.org

ISBN 978-92-9277-722-7 (print); 978-92-9277-723-4 (PDF); 978-92-9277-724-1 (ebook)
Publication Stock No. TCS260087-2
DOI: http://dx.doi.org/10.22617/TCS260087-2

Note:
In this publication, "$" refers to United States dollars.

Cover design by Claudette Rodrigo.

CONTENTS

ACKNOWLEDGMENTS

This publication is a knowledge product of the Asian Development Bank with funding support from the Technical Assistance Special Fund under Technical Assistance 57273 Mongolia: Climate-Smart Mining for a New Climate Economy.

The report was prepared by Soledad Mills, senior vice president; and Assheton Stewart Carter, founder and executive chair, both at TDi Sustainability Inc., under the overall guidance of Dustin Schinn, water resources specialist, Agriculture, Food, Nature, and Rural Development Sector Office, Sectors Department 2.

The report benefited from comments received from Ehsan Khan, director general, East Asia Regional Department (EARD); Shannon Cowlin, country director, Mongolia Resident Mission, EARD; Balabhaskara Reddy Bathula, regional head, Operations Coordination, EARD; Bruce Dunn, head, Office of Safeguards (OSFG); Francesco Ricciardi, senior safeguards specialist (Environment), OSFG; Aaron Sexton, principal safeguards specialist (Environment), OSFG; Dindi Tisha Samsuya, senior safeguards officer (Social), OSFG; Haidy Seang-Ear Dupuy, unit head, NGO and Civil Society Center, Climate Change and Sustainable Development Department; Yothin Jinjarak, senior economist, People's Republic of China Resident Mission, EARD; and Martino Pelli, senior country economist, Mongolia Resident Mission.

The authors are eternally grateful for the inputs and comments received from Mongolia's civil society during a consultation held in Ulaanbaatar in December 2024 and through subsequent iterative reviews of the draft report. The authors further extend their appreciation to the Ministry of Industry and Mineral Resources and the Ministry of Economy and Development of the Government of Mongolia for fruitful cooperation.

John Eric van Zant edited the report, while Abigail Garrovillas, lead operations officer, EARD, and Mary Ann Magadia, operations officer, EARD, provided administrative support.

ABBREVIATIONS

ADB	Asian Development Bank
ESG	environmental, social, and governance
GHG	greenhouse gas
ICMM	International Council on Mining and Metals
ILO	International Labour Organization
OECD	Organisation for Economic Co-operation and Development
SIA	Social Impact Assessment
SOE	state-owned enterprise
UN	United Nations
UNECE	United Nations Economic Commission for Europe
UNESCO	United Nations Educational, Scientific and Cultural Organization

EXECUTIVE SUMMARY

Mongolia has the opportunity to be a leader in sustainable mining practices and a key contributor to the global renewable energy supply chain while ensuring responsible resource management, community engagement, and ecosystem protection and restoration. This initiative would also align well with the country's 2050 Vision, which recognizes mining as a priority economic sector and commits to responsible practices, adheres to international standards, and aims to evolve the mining sector into a globally competitive and responsible part of the economy while minimizing environmental damage.

This report assesses the regulatory framework of Mongolia's mining sector in the context of global environmental, social, and governance (ESG) standards, focusing on how the country can develop a climate-smart and responsible strategy for mining critical minerals required for clean energy technologies. The sector faces several ESG risks that could negatively impact the country's ability to attract investment in critical minerals. This assessment identifies the gaps in Mongolia's mining laws and practices and proposes ways to align with those international standards.

In December 2024, the Asian Development Bank consulted civil society organizations and government stakeholders in Ulaanbaatar to discuss and get feedback on the preliminary results of the draft ESG assessment of the Mongolian mining sector. More than 40 representatives from Mongolian civil society, the Ministry of Environment and Climate Change, and the Ministry of Industry and Mineral Resources participated in the workshop. The consultations provided an opportunity to learn from civil society stakeholders and government representatives in a collaborative dialogue, jointly develop recommendations for ESG risk identification and mitigation in the mining sector, and foster alignment with responsible mining practices, stakeholder engagement, and sustainable resource management. This report incorporates the concerns and recommendations that emerged during the consultations.

Key Findings

Environmental risks. Mongolia's mining policies lack clear regulations on biodiversity conservation, water management, and post-mining land rehabilitation. The absence of mandatory mine closure plans and weak enforcement of environmental impact assessments contribute to ecosystem degradation, water scarcity, and inadequate land restoration practices. Renewable energy integration within mining operations is also not sufficiently promoted, leading to higher greenhouse gas emissions.

Social risks. Mongolia's mining sector faces challenges, including the displacement of communities, labor rights, gender inequality, and the use of child labor in artisanal mining operations. Government policies do not adequately protect vulnerable groups such as women, seminomadic pastoralists and nomadic herders, ethnic minorities, and migrant workers. In addition, no clear guidelines exist for resettlement or benefit-sharing mechanisms with local communities.

Governance gaps. Weak regulatory frameworks, lack of transparency, and poor enforcement of existing laws hinder sustainable development. Governance risks are exacerbated by the potential for corruption, particularly in the allocation of mining licenses and revenue distribution. There are no mandatory stakeholder engagement processes, leaving communities without formal channels to address grievances.

Actionable Recommendations

The report recommends policy in the following three key areas:

(i) **Strengthen environmental regulations.** This refers in particular to biodiversity conservation, water management, post-mining rehabilitation, tailings management, and integrating climate-smart mining practices.

(ii) **Enhance social safeguards.** This should occur around social impact assessments, community consultation and engagement; free, prior, and informed consent; benefit-sharing; labor and health and safety protections; gender-sensitive policies; and artisanal and small-scale mining.

(iii) **Improve governance.** Better governance is required to ensure revenue transparency, anticorruption, revenue-sharing and taxation, and stakeholder engagement. As the country revises its legal frameworks to better align with ESG goals and international standards, the report also recommends that Mongolia strengthen its capacity to enforce and monitor these laws.

1 INTRODUCTION

The global energy transition is generating unprecedented demand for minerals critical in the manufacturing components of clean energy technologies. As countries strive to meet their climate targets and transition to low-carbon economies, critical minerals such as lithium, cobalt, copper, and rare earth elements have become indispensable in technologies like solar panels, wind turbines, and electric vehicles. This demand is expected to soar further, with the International Energy Agency projecting a dramatic increase in the need for these minerals by 2040.[1] Consequently, aligning mining practices with sustainable development goals has become a strategic priority for resource-rich nations, including Mongolia.

The country's mining sector is pivotal to its economic development, with its vast deposits of copper, molybdenum, and rare earth minerals positioning it to supply the world's critical minerals. However, as global demand increases, the country should ensure its mining practices align with responsible, sustainable, and climate-smart principles. This is particularly relevant in the context of its "Vision 2050," which aims to diversify its economy, enhance environmental sustainability, and ensure the responsible extraction and use of its natural resources. The policy presents a unique opportunity to integrate climate-conscious strategies in mining practices, ensuring the nation contributes to the global energy transition while promoting long-term economic stability.

This assessment evaluates existing policies governing the mining sector within the framework of international standards on environmental, social, and governance (ESG) principles. The report identifies gaps and recommends policies to equip the mining industry to responsibly support the global energy transition. As critical minerals become increasingly important for clean energy technologies, this assessment seeks to identify how the Asian Development Bank (ADB) can support Mongolia in leveraging these opportunities while mitigating the social and environmental impacts of mining.

1 International Energy Agency. 2023. *Critical Minerals Market Review 2023*.

2 | METHODOLOGY

Data Collection

The authors collected data through a comprehensive review of the literature, laws, policy documents, and international standards. This included in-depth examination in several areas:

- Mongolian mining regulations and laws, alongside key international frameworks such as the United Nations (UN) Guiding Principles on Business and Human Rights;
- the Extractive Industries Transparency Initiative;
- the Equator Principles;
- the Paris Agreement;
- the Organisation for Economic Co-operation and Development (OECD) Guidelines for Multinational Enterprises;
- the OECD Due Diligence Guidance for Responsible Supply Chains of Minerals from Conflict-Affected and High-Risk Areas; and
- the Voluntary Principles on Security and Human Rights.

The authors consulted publicly available ESG reports from mining operations to identify gaps in the country's regulatory landscape and responsible mining practices.

Analytical Framework

The study's gap analysis compared Mongolia's mining policies against recognized international standards in responsible mining, stakeholder engagement, and ESG criteria. It conducted the assessment based on a detailed evaluation of common ESG risks and impacts associated with mining. Its evaluation focuses on the sector's preparedness for the green transition, emphasizing the integration of renewable energy, climate-smart mining technologies, and sustainable corporate practices.

Civil society widely recognizes the persistent and weak enforcement of environmental and human rights protections and insufficient monitoring in Mongolia.[2] As the country revises its legal frameworks to better align with ESG goals and international standards, it is crucial that it also strengthens its capacity to enforce and monitor these laws. Without better enforcement, even the most progressive policy changes will have a limited impact on the ground.

2 US Department of State. 2023. *2023 Country Reports on Human Rights Practices: Mongolia*.

Civil Society Organization Consultation

In December 2024, ADB consulted civil society organizations and government stakeholders in Ulaanbaatar to gather feedback on the preliminary results of the draft ESG assessment of the mining sector. Through collaborative dialogue involving more than 40 representatives of Mongolian civil society, the Ministry of Environment and Climate Change, and the Ministry of Industry and Mineral Resources, ADB learned from these stakeholders. Together, they developed recommendations for ESG risk identification and mitigation in the mining sector and to align responsible mining practices, stakeholder engagement, and sustainable resource management. The report incorporates the concerns raised and the recommendations of the civil society organizations.

3 KEY MONGOLIAN LAWS RELEVANT TO THE MINING INDUSTRY

Overview

Several laws and policies are important for understanding the regulatory framework's alignment with international ESG standards. These include the Minerals Law of Mongolia (2006), the cornerstone for managing exploration and extraction activities. This law is complemented by licensing regulations under the Law on Minerals, governing the issuance and management of mining licenses.

Article 39 of the Minerals Law requires mining license holders to conduct an environmental impact assessment and prepare an environmental protection plan. The law also mandates that mining companies establish financial reserves to ensure the rehabilitation of mining sites after they are closed (Article 38). Article 42 requires the mineral license holder to have a local cooperation agreement with local administrative bodies. Article 44 obligates mining companies to adhere to health and safety regulations, protecting workers and nearby communities from potential hazards associated with mining activities. The Minerals Law requires companies to sign local-level agreements with local authorities to outline how they will cooperate on environmental protection, infrastructure development, mine use, and employment. The Mongolian Parliament approved the law on the Sovereign Wealth Fund in April 2024, which aims to fairly distribute mineral resource benefits to all citizens. The law also includes amendments to the Minerals Law; most notably, the Government of Mongolia has the authority to seize up to 50% of shares of mining projects without compensation.[3]

The Law on Land, enacted in 1994 and amended several times, is the primary land law in Mongolia. The law governs various aspects of land ownership, possession, and use, and it affirms that the state owns all land and mineral resources. The law outlines the procedures for granting land use rights for various purposes, including mining, and emphasizes environmental protection and sustainable land use.

The Law on Environmental Protection (1995) and the Law on Environmental Impact Assessment (2011) are central to regulating the environmental impacts of mining activities. The Law on Environmental Protection provides a broad framework for natural resource use, mandating the sustainable management of environmental assets. The Environmental

[3] PwC. 2024. *Amendments to the Minerals Law and Related Tax Issues*.

Impact Assessment Law requires mining projects to undergo thorough environmental assessments before commencing operations. Additionally, the Law on Disaster Protection (2017) is invoked for emergency response planning, including coverage of environmental disasters caused by mining. The Law on Petroleum (2014) regulates petroleum exploration, development, and production activities. The Law on Petroleum Products (2005) governs the importation, manufacturing, sale, transportation, and storage of petroleum products, ensuring operational safety.

The Law on Water (2012) and the Law on Water Pollution Payment (2019) provide guidelines for water use, protection, and pollution mitigation in mining activities. Water scarcity in key mining regions, compounded by inadequate enforcement of these laws, remains a pressing issue. The Law on Air (2013) and the National Program on Air Pollution Reduction (2017–2025) address the need to control air pollution in mining operations, particularly the reduction of greenhouse gas emissions.

In the context of climate change and renewable energy integration, Mongolia's Nationally Determined Contribution (2019) and the Law on Renewable Energy (2007) provide the framework for the country's efforts to incorporate renewable energy into mining operations. These laws are bolstered by the National Renewable Energy Program (2015–2030), which sets targets for increasing the use of renewable energy in various sectors, including mining.

The Law on Prohibition of Mineral Exploration and Exploitation in Run-off Source Areas, Protection Zones of Water Bodies and Forested Areas (2009) establishes strict restrictions on mining activities in ecologically sensitive zones to protect water resources and forest ecosystems.

The Regulation on the Temporary and Permanent Closure of Mines (2003) outlines requirements for mine closure planning, emphasizing environmental rehabilitation and sustainable post-mining land use. The Procedures for the Pre-Recovery and Closure of Mines, Mining and Beneficiation Facilities (2019) sets out the rules for creating and implementing a closure management plan for mining sites, processing plants, and related facilities. The goal is to manage closure in line with laws on minerals, environmental impact assessments, and other relevant regulations. The Order of the Minister of Environment, Green Development and Tourism on Approval of Methods for Technical and Biological Rehabilitation of Areas Damaged by Mining Activities (2015) provides guidelines for rehabilitating and restoring land damaged by mining and mineral processing activities and includes policies for cost estimation for restoration efforts.

The Law on Human Rights Defenders, adopted in 2021, aims to protect individuals and groups advocating for human rights, ensuring their safety, freedom from retaliation, and an enabling environment for their work.

Cultural and social protections are also covered under the Law on Protection of Cultural Heritage (2014), which aims to safeguard cultural sites that may be impacted by mining activities.

Artisanal and small-scale mining is governed by amendments to the Law on Minerals (2010), as well as specific regulations like Resolution N. 308, Regulation N. 151 (2017), and Resolution N. 355 (2019), Resolution N. 296 on the Extraction of Minerals by Artisanal and Small-Scale Mining, approved in August 2022,[4] along with the National Action

4 Delve. 2023. *State of the Artisanal and Small-Scale Mining Sector Report*.

Plan (2019–2023), which aims to formalize and regulate artisanal and small-scale mining activities. The Mercury Ban (2007) targets the elimination of mercury use in artisanal and small-scale gold mining.

The governance of financial and revenue matters in Mongolia's mining sector is regulated by several key laws, including the Law on Investment (2013), the Anti-Corruption Law (2006), the General Taxation Law (1992, with amendments in 2020 and 2024), and the Corporate Income Tax Law. Additionally, the Law on the Sovereign Wealth Fund (2019) plays a role in ensuring that mining revenues contribute to long-term economic stability. The Natural Resource Use Payment Law (1995) mandates that revenues from natural resource use payments be allocated to environmental protection and natural resource rehabilitation.

The regulatory framework includes tax laws such as the Business Entity/Corporate Income Tax Law (2019), the Personal Income Tax Law (2019), and the Value Added Tax Law (2015).

Policy Gaps

Despite these regulations, policy gaps remain, particularly in ensuring comprehensive environmental protections, equitable revenue sharing, and effective community engagement in mining decisions. The current regulations lack clear requirements for the restoration of land to its original ecological state or for sustainable post-mining land use.[5] Mining companies lack specific incentives to enable the transition to renewable energy.[6]

Section VII analyzes specific policy gaps related to ESG issues in the context of risks and impacts presented in Section VI. Concerns exist about weak enforcement, particularly compliance with environmental standards; however, data on the implementation of regulations is generally lacking. Civil society organizations have emphasized the lack of enforcement of laws, in particular, of environmental laws and mine closure laws. Also noted was the lack of coordination among government agencies, resulting in gaps in oversight and policy implementation.

5 United Nations Economic Commission for Europe (UNECE). 2018. *Environmental Performance Reviews: Mongolia*.

6 M. Dimovska. 2024. *Mongolia's Clean Energy Transition: Pathway to Sustainable and Inclusive Development*. United Nations Development Programme. 2 January.

4 INTERNATIONAL FRAMEWORKS

Overview

Mongolia has ratified key international conventions related to ESG standards and sustainability, actively participates in global sustainability frameworks, and has endorsed a number of international standards. Notable examples include:

Paris Agreement (2015). The country ratified the Paris Agreement in 2016 and committed to reducing its greenhouse gas emissions by 22.7% by 2030, compared to a business-as-usual scenario. Its nationally determined contribution focuses on energy, agriculture, and waste management. Given its vulnerability to desertification and water scarcity, addressing climate change is critical for Mongolia's development strategy.

Convention on Biological Diversity. The country ratified the Convention on Biological Diversity in 1993, demonstrating its commitment to conserving biodiversity, sustainably using its components, and ensuring the equitable sharing of benefits from genetic resources. Its efforts under the convention focus on protecting its unique ecosystems, addressing threats like land degradation and desertification, and integrating biodiversity considerations into national development strategies.

Kunming-Montreal Global Biodiversity Framework (2022). Mongolia has endorsed the Kunming-Montreal Global Biodiversity Framework, aligning its policies with global goals to halt biodiversity loss and restore degraded ecosystems. The framework emphasizes the role in conserving its unique biodiversity, particularly in combating desertification and land degradation.

Ramsar Convention (1971). Mongolia became a party to the Ramsar Convention in 1998, committing to the conservation and sustainable use of wetlands of international importance. With 11 Ramsar-designated wetlands, including Lake Uvs Nuur and Lake Khuvsgul, the country focuses on protecting critical habitats for biodiversity and maintaining water resource ecosystems.

30x30 Commitment on Protected Areas (2022). Mongolia has pledged to conserve 30% of its land and marine areas by 2030 as part of the global 30x30 initiative to address biodiversity loss. With over 17% of its territory already under formal protection, the country is scaling up efforts to expand conservation areas, especially in ecologically significant regions such as the Gobi Desert.

World Heritage Convention (1972). Mongolia ratified the World Heritage Convention in 1990, recognizing its responsibility to protect the cultural and natural heritage of outstanding universal value. The country has several sites inscribed on the United Nations Educational, Scientific and Cultural Organization (UNESCO) World Heritage List, including the Orkhon Valley Cultural Landscape and the Petroglyphic Complexes of the Mongolian Altai.

Extractive Industries Transparency Initiative. Since joining the initiative in 2007, Mongolia has published detailed reports on revenues from its mining and oil sectors, promoting transparency and accountability. This initiative is vital in a country where mining significantly contributes to the economy.

United Nations Convention against Corruption. Mongolia signed the convention in 2005 and ratified it in 2006.

The United Nations Guiding Principles on Business and Human Rights. Mongolia's National Action Plan (2023–2027) outlines measures to prevent and address human rights abuses in business operations. The plan emphasizes corporate accountability and the need for businesses to adhere to international human rights standards.

OECD Guidelines for Multinational Enterprises. While not an OECD member, Mongolia aligns with many of the OECD Guidelines for responsible business conduct, particularly in mining. The government encourages foreign enterprises to adopt practices that promote sustainable and responsible business practices.[7]

Towards Sustainable Mining Initiative. In October 2024, during Mongolia's National Mining Week, the Mongolian National Mining Association adopted the Towards Sustainable Mining initiative. This performance system, developed by the Mining Association of Canada, aims to enhance environmental and social practices within the mining sector. By implementing Towards Sustainable Mining, companies commit to measuring and publicly reporting the quality of mining management systems, reflecting a dedication to responsible mining.

Governance Programme for Sustainable Natural Resource Management. Mongolia is participating in this initiative of the Swedish Environmental Protection Agency and the United Nations Development Programme. It works with ministries of mining, environment, and other national and local stakeholders to strengthen environmental governance in the mining sector and improve stakeholders' meaningful engagement and mutual responsibility through scaling up participatory environmental monitoring and responsible mining mechanisms.[8]

Mongolia joined the Basel Convention on the Control of Transboundary Movement of Hazardous Wastes in 1997, the Rotterdam Convention on the Prior Informed Consent Procedure for Certain Hazardous Chemicals and Pesticides in International Trade in 2001, and the Minamata Convention on Mercury in 2015.

7 UNECE. 2018. *Environmental Performance Reviews: Mongolia*.
8 Environmental Governance Programme (EGP). *Mongolia*. From the EGP for Sustainable Natural Resource Management.

Policy Gaps

While Mongolia has made progress in its commitment to promoting sustainable development, it has yet to ratify several important international conventions, including:

Convention on the Protection of the Rights of All Migrant Workers and Members of their Families. Mongolia has not ratified this convention, which is designed to protect the rights of migrant workers and their families.

International Labour Organization (ILO) Convention 169—Indigenous and Tribal Peoples Convention. Mongolia has not ratified this ILO convention aimed at protecting the rights of Indigenous and Tribal Peoples, but it has signed the UN Declaration on the Rights of Indigenous Peoples. The country does not officially recognize any groups as Indigenous Peoples under international definitions. Its nomadic herders are often discussed in the context of Indigenous Peoples due to their traditional lifestyles and strong cultural ties to the land. However, they are not formally recognized as Indigenous Peoples under international law or by Mongolia itself, except for the traditionally nomadic reindeer-herding *Tsaatan*, who are described as Indigenous Peoples.[9]

Optional Protocol to the International Covenant on Economic, Social and Cultural Rights. Mongolia is a party to the main covenant, but has not ratified the Optional Protocol, which allows individuals to submit complaints to the UN regarding violations of economic, social, and cultural rights.

9 Minority Rights Group. 2020. *Mongolia*.

5 KEY ENVIRONMENTAL, SOCIAL, AND GOVERNANCE RISKS IN MONGOLIA'S MINING SECTOR

The mining sector is a cornerstone of the economy, contributing significantly to national revenue and employment. However, the industry's rapid expansion has raised ESG concerns. This introduction examines the key risks associated with Mongolian mining, with a focus on environmental degradation, social challenges, and governance deficiencies.

Environmental Risks

The mining sector faces environmental risks due to policy gaps that affect biodiversity, water management, post-mining land use, and waste management. The environmental impact of mining activities, if not properly regulated, can lead to severe degradation of ecosystems, contamination of water resources, and long-lasting harm to the environment. Mongolia ranks 143 out of 180 on the 2024 Environmental Performance Index,[10] suggesting weaknesses in environmental policies, regulations, and enforcement mechanisms.

Biodiversity loss. The country's protected areas cover almost 33 million hectares, or 21% of its national territory.[11] Open-pit mining and infrastructure development (e.g., roads, railways, and mining facilities) have disrupted vast areas of natural habitats. Grasslands and forests, critical ecosystems for wildlife, are being converted into industrial sites, particularly in the Gobi Desert and other mining hotspots. Fragmentation of habitats has negatively affected the movement and genetic diversity of species such as the Mongolian gazelle and snow leopard. Although data is limited, disturbance of protected-area buffer zones by mining activities has been identified by some studies as having adversely affected threatened species that migrate through these areas.[12] The cumulative effects of mining, combined with climate change and overgrazing, pose a severe threat to Mongolia's unique biodiversity. Civil society organizations noted during the consultations that mining in protected areas takes place in contravention of existing laws and with insufficient consultation and planning.

10 The Environmental Performance Index biennially ranks countries on their environmental performance, including on climate change, air and water quality, biodiversity, and waste management. Yale and Columbia universities produce the index based on data from sources, including government agencies, international organizations, and academic institutions.

11 *World Wildlife Fund*. 2020. The Parliament of Mongolia has Approved 10 Areas for National Protected Areas. 8 May.

12 The Nature Conservancy Mongolia Program. 2017. *Identifying Conservation Priorities in the Face of Future Development*; J.D. Farrington. 2009. The Impact of Mining activities on Mongolia's Protected Areas: A Status Report with Policy Recommendations. *Journal of Integrated Environmental Assessment and Management*. 2009. 1 (3). pp. 283–289.

Water management. Mongolia is ranked as 1 of 46 high-water-risk countries in the world.[13] It has faced a severe water shortage over the last decade, and hundreds of Mongolian lakes have dried up in recent years, with much of the southern lands experiencing desertification. Mining accounts for 13% of total water demand and is likely to become a larger water user in the future.[14] Mining operations require a lot of water, which can threaten the water balance in arid and semi-arid regions like the Gobi Desert. The rapid growth of the mining industry in the South Gobi region, where many mining operations are clustered, has made the region a hotspot of water insecurity (footnote 14).

Water extraction for mining draws down near-surface groundwater in the local cone of depression and potentially over large distances depending on groundwater hydrology. This can affect wells, springs, and vegetation productivity, reducing water and forage availability and impacting groundwater-dependent systems.[15] Riverbank erosion and contamination of rivers and groundwater with heavy metals and toxic chemicals (e.g., cyanide and mercury) used in mining have harmed aquatic ecosystems and dependent species.[16] Civil society organizations pointed out that mining operations discharge waste into water systems, affecting human and livestock health.

Land degradation and post-mining land rehabilitation. Land degradation is one of the most serious environmental problems in Mongolia. Land degradation refers to the reduction or loss of biological or economic productivity and complexity of land. The inefficient rehabilitation of land after mining operations clearly is a key environmental risk for the sector. An estimated 100,000 hectares of land have been degraded by coal and gold mining activities. Only a very small part of the land degraded by mining activities has been restored.[17]

Mining-related environmental degradation from soil contamination has become a huge issue for regional ecosystems. Several studies have investigated heavy metals in the soils of the country's biggest cities, particularly in the vicinity of mining areas.[18]

Waste management and tailings. The poor management of mining waste, particularly tailings, is a common environmental risk in large-scale mining operations. Large, open-pit mining activities generate large amounts of waste soil, and ore processing activities, which discharge their waste in tailings facilities. Mongolia has experienced tailings dam failures, with significant environmental and social impacts, with toxic materials contaminating water sources and affecting local communities. Civil society organizations confirmed that tailings breaches have occurred due to lack of enforcement, lack of transparency, and lack of consultation with communities.

13 World Resources Institute. 2023. *Aqueduct Water Risk Atlas Country Rankings*.
14 Asian Development Bank (ADB). 2020. *Making Water in Mongolia Available at the Right Time, at the Right Place, and in the Right Quality*. Brief No. 140.
15 The Nature Conservancy Mongolia Program. 2017. *Identifying Conservation Priorities in the Face of Future Development*.
16 Batbayar, G. et al. 2017. Chemical Water Quality Gradients in the Mongolian Sub-Catchments of the Selenga River Basin. *Journal of Environmental Monitoring and Assessment*. 189 (8); McIntyre, N. et al. 2016. A Multi-Disciplinary Approach to Understanding the Impacts of Mines on Traditional Uses of Water in Northern Mongolia. *Journal of Science of the Total Environment*. 557–558. pp. 404–414.
17 UNECE. 2018. *Environmental Performance Review of Mongolia*.
18 Sodnomdarjaa, E. et al. 2024. Resource Conundrum in Mongolia: Soil Contamination from Coal and Copper-Molybdenum Mining. *Journal of Soil Use and Management*. This reference quotes several studies.

Uncontrolled chemical waste from leachate is a major environmental issue in mining in Mongolia.[19] Under the dry and windy climate during spring and autumn, the exposed sediments of mine tailings become an additional source of anthropogenic windblown dust and pose potential threats to the surrounding environment and human health. Higher soil pollution rates have been found near tailing ponds (footnote 14).

It is estimated that 600 mine sites have been abandoned, and these, and improperly reclaimed mine sites, can cause toxic pollution such as mercury and uranium, which are hazards to humans and animals, who may fall into mine pits, and sources of desertification.[20]

Civil society organizations have noted the issue of dust from the transportation of mine ores and materials to support mining operations, which causes significant environmental impacts in arid ecosystems such as the Gobi Desert, and inadequate engineering solutions for environmental mitigation in the mining sector.

Artisanal and small-scale mining. Artisanal and small-scale mining in Mongolia has environmental impacts, including but not limited to loss of habitat and pasturelands due to land degradation, loss of pasture due to displacement of local herders by artisanal and small-scale mining communities; increased risk of mortality to livestock and wildlife posed by mine shafts and pits; disturbance to wild animals through establishment of new settlements; disruption and pollution of hydrology and biodiversity of streams and rivers by alluvial mine workings; and presence of artisanal and small-scale mining activities adjacent to or within protected areas.[21]

Climate change and emissions. Despite contributing only 0.1% of the global greenhouse gas (GHG) emissions, Mongolia is the 9th highest per capita emitter, due to heavy reliance on coal for energy production. Coal accounts for 70% of the total energy supply.[22] The country faces severe challenges in meeting energy consumption needs and remains highly dependent on energy imports. The country ranks 116 out of 120 countries on the Energy Transition Index, which reflects the significant challenges and a lack of progress in transitioning to renewable energy.[23] A low ranking indicates high dependence on fossil fuels, challenges in ensuring a reliable energy supply, limited investment in and adoption of renewable energy, poor infrastructure for clean energy distribution, and a lack of an energy transition plan. The rapid growth in mining over the last 2 decades has accelerated emissions, due to the carbon intensity of the sector and reliance on coal-fired power plants as the primary energy source.

Social Risks

Mongolia's mining sector is challenged by a range of negative social impacts that threaten sustainable development and social cohesion.

Displacement and loss of livelihoods. Mining operations often require large tracts of land, potentially leading to displacement or tensions with local communities. A lack of transparent engagement with communities alongside rushed resettlement and impacts on pasture resources has resulted in a growing number of complaints and court cases, as well as public outcry from households directly

19 World Resources Institute. 2023. *Aqueduct Water Risk Atlas Country Rankings*.
20 United Nations Development Programme Mongolia. 2019. *Training Manual on Responsible Mining*.
21 Wildlife Science and Conservation Center of Mongolia. 2014. *Biodiversity and Artisanal and Small-scale Mining in Mongolia*.
22 World Bank. 2024. *Mongolia Country Climate and Development Report: Overview*.
23 World Economic Forum. 2024. *Fostering Effective Energy Transition 2024*.

impacted by forced displacement and the lack of information about planned development in their places of residence.[24]

Many mining projects are in rural areas where pastoralism and agriculture are primary livelihoods. The expansion of mining activities frequently displaces herders and farmers, disrupting traditional livelihoods and forcing communities to relocate, often without adequate compensation or support for resettlement. This creates tension between mining companies and local communities, with displaced populations facing increased poverty and vulnerability.[25]

For nomadic herders in particular, land displacement and the loss of access to grazing lands due to mining operations have profound social, cultural, and economic consequences.[26] About 70% of Mongolia's land is used for livestock grazing, and nomadic herders practice rotational grazing, allowing their animals to access different vegetation suited for seasonal conditions. This strategy ensures the survival of both the livestock and the herders in the country's harsh climate, with specific grazing lands reserved for difficult winters and breeding periods.[27]

However, mining activities are encroaching on these vital resources, with many mining sites established near water sources crucial to humans and animals. These have led to "land tacking," in which herders are losing access to seasonal migration routes and grazing lands, which are often taken without proper acknowledgment or compensation, due to mining. Rural pastureland is state property, and industrial licensing for mineral extraction overrides herders' traditional rights to mobile land use.[28] The disruption of pastoral routes and the degradation of grazing areas due to mining activities can result in the loss of livestock, which is the primary asset for many rural households.

The lack of legal recognition for herders' land rights exacerbates the issue, as they have no official documents to claim ownership of their grazing lands. In response, recent voluntary rangeland use agreements between herders and local authorities have been implemented, which include provisions for compensation if land is used for mining. However, the effectiveness of these agreements is hampered by poor enforcement, corruption, and inadequate legislative protections. The absence of effective compensation mechanisms or livelihood restoration programs exacerbates these impacts, leaving affected communities worse off. Civil society organizations emphasized these points during the consultation and suggested that nomadic herders be treated as Indigenous Peoples when applying free, prior, and informed consent requirements.

Additionally, civil society organizations noted that mining operations often disregard Mongolia's nomadic traditions and cultural beliefs about land and nature. In 2024, UNESCO registered Mongol nomad migration and associated practices as world intangible cultural heritage.[29] Therefore, impacts on nomadic herders should also be considered as cultural heritage impacts and be avoided, mitigated, and managed to ensure preservation of the nomadic herders' way of life.

---

24 T. Sternberg and A. Alhearn. 2023. Mongolian Mining Engagement with SIA and ESG Initiatives. *Journal of Environmental Impact Assessment Review*. 103.
25 U. Dovchin and S. Dovchin. 2024. The Discourse of the Anthropocene and Posthumanism: Mining-Induced Loss of Traditional Land and the Mongolian Nomadic Herders. *Journal of Ethnicities*. 24 (4).
26 University of Oxford. n.d. *Mitigating the Impact of Mining in Mongolia*.
27 Colorado State University. 2017. *Community-Based Rangeland Management in Mongolia: Outcomes and Keys to Success*. Mongolian Rangelands and Resilience (MOR2) Project.
28 Land Portal. 2022. *Mining Fractures Land and Community in Mongolia*.
29 UNESCO. 2024. *Mongol Nomad Migration and Its Associated Practices*.

Labor rights. The mining sector in Mongolia faces several challenges in respecting labor rights, impacting workers across various types of operations.[30] Those employed by smaller or informal mining companies often endure poor working conditions characterized by inadequate health and safety measures. The lack of protective equipment and training significantly heightens the risk of accidents, resulting in injuries or even fatalities.[31]

In larger industrial mining operations, there are also concerning reports regarding worker safety. Employees frequently face unsafe working environments, excessive working hours, and insufficient wages, highlighting a systemic issue within the sector.[32] Although the country's regulatory framework includes labor protections aimed at ensuring safe and fair working conditions, international reports suggest that enforcement remains weak (footnote 34). The remote nature of mining exacerbates this issue.

Migrant workers, who often relocate from rural regions or neighboring countries to seek employment in the mining sector, are particularly vulnerable. They may encounter precarious employment conditions, including exploitation and limited access to legal protections or recourse in the event of rights violations.[33] The civil society organizations noted that such labor practices are common in mining operations and highlighted issues such as wage reductions post-coronavirus disease; poor working conditions; and negative social, cultural, and economic impacts of migrant worker populations on local communities.

Gender inequality. While women are involved in various capacities within the mining sector, they often find themselves in lower-paying and less secure positions, with limited access to decision-making roles.[34] Many women are confined to informal or auxiliary jobs, such as processing minerals or providing support services to male workers, which tend to offer minimal economic benefits and increase their vulnerability.

Moreover, women in mining communities frequently experience the social and economic disruptions associated with mining activities.[35] The influx of male workers into these areas has been correlated with heightened rates of gender-based violence and the spread of diseases such as HIV/AIDS (footnote 35). Additionally, the environmental degradation linked to mining, particularly the depletion of water resources, disproportionately affects women, who are typically responsible for water collection for their households.

Child labor. The minimum age for work provisions does not meet international standards because they do not provide penalties for violations of these provisions.[36] Child labor—especially at artisanal and small-scale mining sites—is known in the country's mining sector. In informal mining operations, children are frequently exposed to dangerous tools, heavy machinery, and toxic substances like mercury, all of which pose health risks. The use of mercury can result in severe neurological and developmental damage. The ILO has classified child labor in mining as one of the worst forms of such labor due to the extensive physical and

30 United Nations Development Programme (UNDP). 2022. *Business and Human Rights: National Baseline Assessment (Mongolia)*.
31 International Labour Organization. 2016. *Briefing Note: Occupational Safety and Health in Mining in Mongolia*.
32 United States Agency for International Development. 2021. LandLinks. *Mongolia Country Profile*.
33 Asian Development Bank. 2020. Mongolia: Labor Migration and Employment in the Mining Sector.
34 UNDP. 2024. *Gender Equality and Women's Empowerment in Leadership*.
35 Action Research Report. 2014. Mapping Gender-Based Violence and Mining Infrastructure in Mongolian Mining Communities.
36 United States Department of Labor: Bureau of International Labor Affairs. 2023. *Child Labor and Forced Labor Reports: Mongolia*.

psychological harm it causes. Children working in these hazardous environments often face long hours, poor working conditions, and the absence of proper safety measures.

As the mining industry continues to grow in Mongolia, children, particularly girls, are reportedly at increased risk of commercial sexual exploitation and forced labor in artisanal and small-scale mining.[37] Girls are vulnerable to exploitation in nightclubs near mining towns and solicitation for cross-border sex trafficking while their parents are on extended shift rotations (footnote 37).

Inequitable distribution of economic benefits. Mining in Mongolia can generate economic benefits, but these are often unevenly distributed, exacerbating social inequalities. While large-scale mining operations contribute to national revenues, many local communities in mining regions remain impoverished, with limited access to the wealth generated from mining activities. This can lead to social unrest, as communities that bear the brunt of environmental and social impacts see few tangible benefits in employment, infrastructure, or social services.

In many cases, revenues from mining are not effectively channeled into local development projects, and local governments lack the capacity or resources to implement programs that benefit mining-affected communities. This situation is compounded by corruption and mismanagement, which can prevent the use of mining revenues for the public good. Civil society organizations emphasized these points during consultations and noted that compensation frameworks are inequitable.

Efforts to address these social risks should focus on creating mechanisms to ensure that mining revenues are equitably distributed and that local communities, particularly those most affected by mining operations, receive tangible benefits. This includes improving local infrastructure, healthcare, and education, as well as ensuring that mining companies invest in local development through social investment initiatives.

Health and safety impacts. Mining operations carry health and safety risks for workers and surrounding communities. Workers in the mining sector face health issues, including respiratory diseases resulting from exposure to dust and hazardous chemicals. Injuries from accidents are common in both large industrial operations and smaller mining activities.

Communities living near mining sites also risk exposure to environmental pollutants, including heavy metals and chemicals used in extraction and processing.[38] Contaminated water sources and soil degradation can lead to long-term health problems, such as increased incidences of cancer and respiratory illness.

Governance Risks

Mongolia's mining sector faces a complex array of governance risks, which pose challenges to sustainable development and responsible resource management. These risks stem from weak regulatory frameworks, poor enforcement of existing laws, and gaps in transparency and accountability mechanisms, creating an environment where corruption and inefficiencies can thrive.[39] These issues, when unaddressed, undermine the sector's contribution to economic development and exacerbate social and environmental harms.

---

37 US Department of Labor. 2020. *Findings on the Worst Forms of Child Labor: Mongolia*.
38 International Labour Organization. 2016. *Mongolia Briefing Note: Occupational Safety and Health in Mining*.
39 World Bank. 2020. *Mongolia's Mining Sector: Managing the Future*.

Weak regulatory frameworks and enforcement. A primary governance challenge in the mining sector is the lack of a strong, coherent regulatory framework.[40] Although the country has implemented several laws and policies aimed at managing the mining industry, including the Mineral Law and the Law on Environmental Protection, enforcement remains inconsistent. Civil society organizations noted that this is exacerbated by incoherent laws and conflicting mandates between different government agencies, from policy formulation to implementation. Regulatory bodies are often under-resourced and lack the technical capacity to effectively monitor and regulate mining activities. This weak enforcement leads to noncompliance with environmental and safety standards, as well as a failure to adequately protect workers' rights.

Moreover, the decentralized nature of the governance system contributes to regulatory gaps, where local authorities often lack the capacity or resources to implement national policies at the community level. This disconnect between national and local governance leads to fragmented oversight and an increase in unregulated, informal mining activities, particularly in rural areas.

Civil society organizations pointed out that licensing processes lack transparency and accountability, with over 2,000 active mines operating under unclear standards, and that exploration licenses are being transferred into mining licenses without proper gatekeeping. They also noted that the lack of enforcement of laws and standards is not only an issue with the government, but also with investors, companies, and multilateral development banks.

Corruption and lack of transparency. Corruption is a challenge in Mongolia, stemming from political corruption, wide-reaching immunity for officials, and lack of transparency in procurement processes.[41] During the consultation, civil society organizations noted that many mining projects are operated by or in partnership with state-owned enterprises (SOEs), which have a record of governance issues and corruption. The Corruption Perceptions Index 2023 by Transparency International ranks Mongolia 121st out of 180 countries.[42] The country faces notable deficiencies in implementation and compliance with anticorruption laws, transparency, and accountability for noncompliance, as well as lack of protection of whistleblowers.[43] Corruption is a governance risk in its mining sector, with pervasive issues surrounding the awarding of mining licenses and contracts.[44]

Corruption within the country SOEs in the mining sector is a major concern. The state holds stakes in many large mining operations, and governance within these SOEs is often weak, lacking clear lines of accountability.[45] Without proper oversight, SOEs can become vehicles for political patronage, corruption, and inefficiency, which ultimately erodes the sector's capacity to contribute positively to the economy.

40 Environmental Impact Assessment Review. 2023. *Mongolian Mining Engagement with SIA and ESG Initiatives*.
41 Transparency International. n.d. *Country Profile: Mongolia*.
42 Transparency International. 2023. *Corruption Perceptions Index: Mongolia*.
43 Transparency International Mongolia. 2024. Civil Society Report on the Implementation of the UN Convention Against Corruption in Mongolia.
44 OECD. 2015. *Anti-Corruption Reforms in Mongolia*.
45 Open Government Partnership. 2019. *Mongolia: Improve Governance of State Owned Enterprises*.

Lack of transparency in the management of the mining sector, particularly in revenue distribution and allocation of mining licenses, hinders public scrutiny and allows misallocation of resources, further entrenching governance failures. In numerous cases, unclear or corrupt practices in the awarding of mining contracts has led to public distrust and accusations of favoritism or corruption.[46]

The Extractive Industries Transparency Initiative, which as noted Mongolia joined in 2007, has helped improve transparency in areas such as revenue reporting. However, a lack of transparency in beneficial ownership—the individuals who ultimately control mining companies—has been a persistent challenge. Without clear disclosures, it is difficult to identify conflicts of interest or prevent corrupt practices, where politically connected individuals may unfairly benefit from mining projects (footnote 44).

Stakeholder engagement and social license to operate. Effective governance in the mining sector requires meaningful engagement with local communities and stakeholders. In Mongolia, the failure to adequately involve local populations in decision-making processes exacerbates tensions between mining companies and communities.[47] During the consultations, civil society organizations emphasized that the limited involvement of herders and local communities in decision-making processes exacerbates conflicts and advocated for equitable participation and stronger grievance mechanisms.

Many communities, particularly those in remote areas, experience negative impacts from mining activities, such as environmental degradation, water contamination, and displacement, without seeing corresponding benefits in employment or local development. The absence of robust consultation mechanisms with local communities can lead to conflicts, protests, and even the suspension of mining operations, which hurts both companies and communities.

46 Natural Resource Governance Institute. 2023. Diagnosing Corruption in the Extractives Sector: Mongolia Case Study.

47 Natural Resource Governance Institute. 2024. *Scoping Study on Extractive Sector State Owned Enterprise Disclosures in Mongolia*; Intergovernmental Forum on Mining, Minerals, Metals and Sustainable Development (IGF). 2017. IGF Mining Policy Framework Assessment: Mongolia; B. Dalaibuyan. 2022. Negotiating the Coexistence of Mining and Pastoralism in Mongolia. *Journal of Contemporary East Asia Studies*. 11 (1). pp. 6–63.

6 IDENTIFIED POLICY GAPS

Environmental Policy Gaps

Mongolia's environmental policies covering the mining sector reveal several gaps, particularly in environmental impact assessments, biodiversity protection, water management, post-mining land use, and climate mitigation and adaptation. Environmental impact assessments are conducted late in the permitting process, after the issuance of the special mining license, although before the issuance of the permit to start mining operations. Civil society organizations reiterated this concern during the consultation and highlighted that the assessments do not involve communities and the results are not made available to affected stakeholders. The cumulative impact assessment instrument, although provided for in the 2012 Law on Environmental Impact Assessment, is not used.[48] Furthermore, although the Law on Environmental Protection addresses biodiversity, it lacks specific mechanisms to ensure biodiversity conservation in mining areas.

The country's Law on Water and the Law on Water Pollution Payment address water management, but these laws do not include comprehensive measures for sustainable water use by mining companies. Clear limits or conditions for water extraction are absent, leading to potential overuse and depletion of water resources. Mongolia should introduce water use regulations specific to the mining industry. Strengthening legal provisions on water management would ensure mining activities do not jeopardize local water supplies.

Post-mining land use and rehabilitation are also inadequately addressed in Mongolian law. The current legal framework for mining closure activity is too general and vague, which enables companies to circumvent their obligations toward local authorities concerning rehabilitation of affected areas (footnote 53). Current regulations lack clear criteria for the rehabilitation of land following the closure of mining operations.

Mongolia has comprehensive legal frameworks in place for addressing emergency response and risk management in mining, as mining companies are required to conduct disaster risk assessments at both national and local levels. Disaster risk assessments are required for strategy and highlight critical facilities, including mining operations, every 3 years or sooner if conditions demand. These assessments follow the guidelines established by the International Standards Organization (ISO) 31000:2020 for risk management. The law further stipulates

[48] UNECE. 2018. *Environmental Performance Reviews: Mongolia*.

that mining companies must carry out detailed disaster risk assessments through licensed entities; however, there is a lack of explicit requirements for stakeholder consultation on the risk assessments. While the Law on Disaster Protection requires stakeholder consultations for risk assessments at various levels, including the community level, it is not prescriptive enough to ensure the quality and inclusiveness of consultations.

The country's mining policy does not provide sufficient guidance or regulation for the management of tailings and other mining waste. Its current guidelines for tailings storage and disposal do not adequately address the long-term containment of hazardous materials, posing risks of soil contamination and water pollution. Additionally, mandatory monitoring systems for tailings facilities are lacking, which increases the likelihood of environmental disasters, such as dam failures or toxic leaks.

Furthermore, mining regulations do not sufficiently address climate mitigation or emissions reduction strategies. The country's mining regulations do not include specific strategies for mitigating the mining sector's carbon footprint or promoting the use of renewable energy. No incentives or regulations are aimed at reducing reliance on fossil fuel-based energy or transitioning to cleaner energy alternatives.

Similarly, the Law on Petroleum lacks provisions for promoting renewable energy within the petroleum supply chain, and there is no encouragement for developing alternative fuels such as biofuels. The law does not impose any requirements for petroleum operators to minimize carbon emissions or integrate renewable energy technologies into their operations. There are no mandates for energy transition plans, carbon pricing, or offsets for emissions generated during petroleum extraction and refining.

Social Policy Gaps

Social impact assessments are not comprehensively required under Mongolian law for all mining projects in the mining approval or risk management processes. The Law on Minerals makes no direct reference to a social impact assessment. Many mining projects proceed without a thorough analysis of the potential social impacts on local communities.

Mongolia's labor laws, while providing general safety provisions, lack mining-specific protections, leaving workers vulnerable to hazards. The Law on Labor Safety and Hygiene fails to address risks unique to the mining sector, such as poor underground ventilation and dangers like cave-ins and explosions. Additionally, occupational diseases related to mining, such as respiratory illnesses, are not comprehensively addressed, leaving long-term health impacts poorly managed.

Mongolia's health and safety laws focus heavily on corrective measures after accidents occur, rather than prioritizing preventive actions like regular risk assessments. This reactive approach leaves mining operations exposed to evolving risks, heightening the danger for workers. Enforcement mechanisms are also weak, with fines for safety violations set too low to deter noncompliance. As a result, companies may not feel compelled to adhere to safety regulations, perpetuating unsafe working conditions.

The legal framework does not meet several international standards to protect children. The Labor Code, which sets a minimum age of 16 to "enter into an employment agreement," does not apply to children in the informal sector or to those who are self-employed. Mongolia's minimum age for work provisions do not meet international standards because they do not provide penalties for violations of these provisions. While Mongolian law allows for penalties for certain forms of child labor that are "detrimental," there is no penalty for working under the minimum age in general. Additionally, the current legal framework provides limited protection for workers in the mining industry, particularly vulnerable groups such as women and migrant laborers.

The country's mining laws lack gender-sensitive language in many national mining laws. In artisanal and small-scale mining regulation, the gender perspective is not considered in Regulation N. 296 on the Extraction of Minerals by Artisanal and Small-Scale Mining. Policies surrounding social protections for women in this area of mining are limited, leaving them vulnerable to gender-based violence, poor working conditions, and economic exclusion. Coverage in these areas in policies is insufficient to provide social safety nets and protections, especially for women facing the double burdens of domestic and mining work.

Mongolia lacks a clear regulatory framework to manage the relationship between large-scale mining and artisanal and small-scale mining, particularly in terms of resource allocation, land use, and environmental protection. Current resource allocation laws do not adequately define equitable access to mineral resources for both sectors, leading to potential conflicts. Land use planning is insufficiently developed to designate specific zones for large-scale mining and artisanal and small-scale mining, which results in land use disputes and operational interference. There is also an absence of policies that formally recognize community rights in mining areas, and no mechanisms are in place to facilitate conflict resolution between large-scale and artisanal and small-scale mining. Technical assistance programs in which large-scale mining supports artisanal and small-scale mining through capacity building and partnerships for resource sharing and joint ventures are also underdeveloped. This limits opportunities for cooperation and mutual benefit.

Community consultation is inadequately addressed in Mongolian law. Although some laws, such as the Law on Disaster Protection, the Environmental Protection Law, and the Law on Minerals, contain provisions that reference the need for community consultation, the laws fall short of mandating comprehensive or systematic engagement. The Environmental Protection Law mentions that citizens have the right to access information about the environment and to participate in environmental protection activities. However, the law does not outline detailed requirements for involving local communities in decision-making processes about mining projects. The Law on Minerals provides for consultation with local government authorities and encourages coordination with local communities when developing environmental management plans. However, the law does not establish clear guidelines for inclusive and meaningful consultations with all impacted community members.

Mongolia lacks clear policies on resettlement. While the Law on Minerals requires mining license holders to compensate private or public landowners for damage to property, including costs related to relocating dwellings or other structures affected by mining operations, it does not provide detailed guidelines on how resettlement should be carried out. The law specifies that compensation must be agreed upon between the mining company and the affected party. In cases where agreements cannot be reached, the law suggests that the matter should be resolved through legal means, which could involve courts. This framework, while offering some level of protection for property, leaves gaps in ensuring that resettlement is conducted in a socially responsible manner, particularly in regard to fair compensation, the process of resettlement, alternative livelihoods and vulnerable groups (groups who may be disproportionately impacted by displacement due to mining activities).

The Law on Minerals provisions for benefit-sharing are limited. It focuses primarily on the rights and obligations of mining license holders, including environmental management and compliance with local regulations, but does not mandate any specific revenue-sharing mechanisms between mining companies and local communities. Article 33 of the law does require mining companies to consult and coordinate with local government authorities for environmental protection and development of infrastructure, but stops short of establishing a formal benefit-sharing framework that directly transfers financial benefits from mining operations to local communities. The laws are more focused on compensating for damages or environmental impacts, rather than creating a framework that ensures sustainable economic benefits for communities from mining profits. During the consultation, civil society organizations asserted an urgent need for improved revenue-sharing mechanisms to benefit local communities and to strengthen governance.

The Ministry of Mining with World Bank support introduced community development agreements to ensure more equitable distribution of mining benefits, improve governance, and restore investor confidence by establishing agreements between local authorities and mining companies. However, their adoption and effectiveness vary significantly across regions and they have been criticized for limited community involvement and short-term implementation.

Governance Policy Gaps

Mongolia's tax laws within the mining sector have gaps related to transparency, accountability, stakeholder engagement, taxation and revenue sharing, and social investment. While the mining industry plays a vital role in the economy, the absence of robust transparency mechanisms limits public access to information on how tax revenues from mining are managed and distributed. Current tax laws, including the Corporate Income Tax, Personal Income Tax, and Value Added Tax, lack public-facing disclosure requirements for tax contributions by mining companies.

Stakeholder engagement and grievance mechanisms are also notably absent in the country's tax and mining legislation. The tax laws fail to provide a framework for engaging local communities, especially those directly impacted by mining activities, or for establishing formal grievance mechanisms. This omission leaves affected communities without formal channels to raise concerns or address conflicts related to tax practices or the social and environmental impacts of mining operations.

Taxation and revenue sharing also present governance challenges in Mongolia. While there are mechanisms to collect taxes from mining companies, there is limited transparency regarding how these revenues are allocated, particularly at the local level. The tax laws do not outline any revenue-sharing mechanisms to ensure that mining profits benefit the regions where operations take place. Civil society organizations also noted that mining royalties and taxation often do not support local development in mining areas.

Finally, social investment in affected communities is not sufficiently regulated or incentivized under the tax laws. There are no tax incentives or obligations for mining companies to engage in social investment activities, such as creating community development funds or contributing to local infrastructure, education, or health services. While some companies voluntarily undertake social investment initiatives, legal requirements and guidelines in terms of structuring and reporting social investment efforts and spending are lacking.

7 RECOMMENDATIONS FOR A RESPONSIBLE MINING STRATEGY

Environmental Recommendations

To address the identified gaps in mining policies, Mongolia should improve the regulation of environmental management of mining operations. First, the country should require environmental impact assessments to be conducted earlier in the permitting process and ensure the cumulative impact assessment instrument is applied. Additionally, the government should establish provisions to ensure the involvement of affected stakeholders and communities in conducting environmental impact assessments and communicating the results. It should support participatory environmental monitoring. For example, as part of the Environmental Governance Programme, a participatory environmental monitoring committee in Airag, Dornogobi Province, has been established that facilitates dialogue between local herders impacted by mining activities and mining companies. These stakeholders have agreed to rehabilitate all remaining pits around the Khongor Ovoo area and to conduct a new environmental impact assessment with the active participation of community members.[49]

Civil society organizations also suggested strengthening the environmental impact assessment process to include community involvement, cumulative impact assessments, and health impact assessments, in particular, in relation to water use and land use by livestock and communities. Environmental impact assessments should be aligned with international standards to ensure quality and comprehensiveness.

Stronger regulations for biodiversity conservation should be introduced, requiring mining companies to avoid mining in buffer zones of protected areas; to conduct biodiversity impact assessments; to implement the mitigation hierarchy, including biodiversity offsets, although civil society organizations noted concerns with how such offsets have been applied in Mongolia; and to develop biodiversity action plans that aim to achieve a net positive gain of biodiversity. Civil society organizations suggested that sensitive ecosystems, such as Ramsar sites and habitats for endangered species, should be off-limits for mining. The International Council on Mining and Metals' Nature Position Statement provides a framework for

49 Environmental Governance Programme (EGP) *Mongolia*. From the EGP for Sustainable Natural Resource Management .

establishing expectations of mining companies for environmental stewardship, which can inform the country's approach to align with international best practices and ensure the protection of local ecosystems.[50]

Mongolia should strengthen its water management by setting clear limits on water extraction and enforcing sustainable practices. It should consider requiring ongoing monitoring to ensure the sustainability of its water sources in mining regions. It should also develop a water stress risk map of the country to identify areas of high water risk and include additional water stewardship requirements for companies operating in water-stressed areas.

The government should also accelerate the implementation of the water pollution fee by enhancing the systematic monitoring of polluting activities and conduct a review of how water usage fees are collected and redistributed to improve the system.

The country should adopt clearer requirements for mining companies on tailings design, construction, operation, monitoring, and closure, in line with international best practices such as the Global Industry Standard on Tailings Management. The government should establish a tailings risk assessment to identify and classify tailings facilities based on risk levels, and increase the frequency of inspections for high-risk facilities. The introduction of mandatory risk assessment and emergency response plans would ensure that mining companies are better prepared to manage environmental risks and mitigate potential disasters such as tailings dam failures. Civil society organizations also recommended establishing more detailed laws and policies on waste management, including hazardous waste and tailings.

Post-mining land use and rehabilitation plans should legally obligate mining companies to restore land to its natural state or repurpose it for sustainable agricultural or other productive uses. This would ensure long-term sustainable land use and minimize environmental degradation. The financial reserves that mining companies are required to establish to ensure adequate rehabilitation of mining sites after their closure should be reviewed to determine whether these funds are sufficient for financing the required reclamation activities in such a way that they meet the existing international best practices in the mining sector. Civil society organizations recommended strengthening the enforcement of environmental laws, including mandatory mine closure and rehabilitation plans that prioritize in situ offsets and include sufficient financial bonding.

Mongolia should strengthen its regulatory framework to address the climate impacts of its mining sector by setting measurable carbon emissions reduction targets and encouraging the integration of renewable energy into mining operations. To align with global standards, the framework should include provisions for monitoring and reducing GHG emissions, making GHG emissions data available for the sector, incorporating renewable energy into mining operations, and adopting carbon capture and storage technologies. The country should require mining companies to develop and disclose Paris-aligned emissions reduction plans.

Drawing from international practices such as the International Council on Mining and Metals' Climate Change Position Statement and the Sustainable Development Goals, the country should require its mining operations to transition toward renewable energy sources

50 International Council on Mining and Metals (ICMM). 2024. Position Statement: Nature.

and encourage policies that support a broader shift toward cleaner energy, reducing reliance on petroleum products.[51] As the country develops its renewable energy infrastructure, it may consider colocating clean energy with mining operations to support its emissions reduction. Such infrastructure investment could be cofinanced by mining companies and international partners.

Incorporating climate action into mining laws and mandating emissions reductions will position Mongolia in line with international climate agreements. Incentives, such as tax breaks for clean energy investments, can accelerate this transition. Civil society organizations suggested integrating climate risks into mining strategies in line with Mongolia's nationally determined contributions, prioritizing cross-sector coordination, and adopting climate risk assessments for strategic projects. They also suggested encouraging the reuse and recycling of minerals to reduce reliance on virgin resources.

In addition to domestic policy reforms, the country should secure international funding and technical assistance to support the transition to sustainable mining practices. Financial mechanisms, such as green bonds or grants, can help companies invest in renewable energy solutions like wind and solar. The country should also require mining companies to measure, verify, and report their GHG emissions in line with its Vision 2050 environmental objective 6.4 to develop a low-carbon, productive, and inclusive green economy.[52]

By integrating climate change commitments, such as the Paris Agreement, into the mining sector's regulations and providing strong incentives for renewable energy adoption, Mongolia can reduce the sector's reliance on coal and lower its emissions. This dual focus on regulatory reform and financial incentives will align the mining industry with its national climate goals as established in its nationally determined contributions and Vision 2050.

Social Recommendations

Mongolia should introduce a mandatory Social Impact Assessment (SIA) in the mining approval process and throughout the mining life cycle for all mining projects to identify and mitigate any negative effects on local populations. SIAs and communicating the results should involve affected stakeholders and communities. Civil society organizations also suggested requiring SIAs, including human rights impact assessments, and ensuring community involvement in impact identification and reporting of results. The Intergovernmental Forum on Mining, Minerals, Metals and Sustainable Development provides further guidance and case studies on international best practices in legal frameworks for environmental and social impact assessment and related management plans for large-scale mines.[53]

Establishing stakeholder engagement and grievance mechanisms at the project level can help to identify and mitigate risks to communities before they become impacts. Civil society organizations also highlighted the need to ensure that effective grievance mechanisms are implemented in mining projects. Mongolia should create formal, legally mandated channels for local communities, particularly those affected by mining operations, to voice concerns and resolve disputes with mining companies. These mechanisms would foster conflict prevention and ensure grievances

51 ICMM. 2021. Position Statement: Climate Change.

52 Government of Mongolia. 2020. *Vision 2050: Environment*.

53 Intergovernmental Forum on Mining, Minerals, Metals and Sustainable Development. 2020. *Guidance for Governments: Improving Legal Frameworks For Environmental and Social Impact Assessment and Management*. International Institute for Sustainable Development.

are addressed efficiently. Companies that have integrated formal grievance mechanisms have seen improvements in company-community relations, reducing tensions and promoting more inclusive governance.[54]

Opportunities to strengthen stakeholder engagement, in particular, community engagement in mining policies include establishing requirements for community consultation in the mining permitting and impact assessment phases, requiring consultation and engagement throughout the mine life cycle, promoting participatory monitoring, requiring companies to establish project-level grievance mechanisms, requiring worker and community consultation in closure planning. The Intergovernmental Forum on Mining, Minerals, Metals and Sustainable Development provides guidance and case studies on how consultation and engagement can be integrated into legal frameworks regulating environmental and social impact assessments and mining which can help align Mongolia's policies with international best practice.[55] Strengthening community participation will enhance trust between stakeholders and mining companies, leading to more equitable and sustainable outcomes.

Civil society organizations emphasized the need to implement culturally sensitive approaches to consultation and engagement, incorporating nomadic traditions and local livelihoods to ensure herders' voices are heard, and the need to ensure equitable compensation mechanisms that consider all affected communities. One model discussed was the creation of tripartite councils involving government, the private sector, and communities to foster trust and accountability.

The government should also consider incorporating free, prior, and informed consent in mining policies, particularly in areas where Indigenous Peoples, seminomadic pastoralists and nomadic herder communities are affected. Civil society organizations also suggested recognizing nomadic herders as Indigenous Peoples. By establishing legal requirements for meaningful consultation with local communities, Mongolia can ensure that mining companies gain the social license to operate while respecting the rights of traditional, land-dependent communities.

It is recommended that Mongolia introduce a formal benefit-sharing framework into its mining laws. This could include mandating mining companies to establish community development funds or directly allocate a portion of mining revenues to local governments and communities. The funds could be used to improve infrastructure, healthcare, education, and other community services in mining-affected areas. Additionally, the government could require companies to engage in partnerships with local stakeholders to design and implement long-term development projects, ensuring that the benefits of resource extraction contribute to the sustainable development of local economies. Independent oversight mechanisms should also be introduced to ensure transparency and accountability in how the benefits are distributed.

To address the gaps in Mongolia's legal framework on resettlement, it is recommended that the government introduce comprehensive resettlement policies that ensure the protection and fair treatment of displaced communities. These policies should include guidelines for fair compensation, calculated based on the full social, economic, and cultural costs of

54 ICMM. 2019. Handling and Resolving Local-level Concerns and Grievances: Human Rights in the Mining and Metals Sector. 10 December.
55 Intergovernmental Forum on Mining, Minerals, Metals and Sustainable Development. 2023. *The Importance of Consultation and Engagement in Environmental and Social Impact Assessments*. IGF Case Study.

displacement, rather than just property value. Additionally, policies should mandate that resettlement plans be developed in consultation with affected communities, ensuring their active participation in decision-making processes. Special attention must be given to vulnerable groups, with provisions for livelihood restoration programs to help displaced individuals transition to alternative income-generating activities. Finally, independent oversight mechanisms should be established to monitor the resettlement process, ensuring that compensation and relocation efforts are transparent, equitable, and compliant with international best practices.

To improve labor conditions in Mongolia's mining sector, it is recommended that the government strengthen its labor protections by addressing gaps in its current legal framework and aligning with international standards, particularly those set by the ILO. Mongolia's existing labor laws, while providing general safety provisions, lack mining-specific health and safety protections, leaving workers vulnerable to hazards unique to the sector. The Law on Labor Safety and Hygiene does not adequately address important risks, such as poor underground ventilation, cave-ins, and explosions, which are key concerns of mining operations. A shift toward proactive measures, such as regular risk assessments, should be prioritized over the current focus on corrective actions after accidents occur. To ensure worker safety, mining-specific protections need to be incorporated into the legal framework. It is recommended that fines for safety violations be increased to deter noncompliance, as the current penalties are too low to compel companies to adhere to safety regulations. In line with best international practices, mining companies should be mandated to conduct regular risk assessments and implement preventive safety measures to protect workers from occupational hazards.

The government should also increase its inspection capacity in line with the sector's projected growth to ensure a sufficient number of inspectors with the requisite expertise to conduct monitoring effectively. This could be supported by technical assistance and partnerships with countries with more mature mining sectors, where inspectors could go for training to observe best practices in mining health and safety.

Long-term occupational health risks, such as respiratory illnesses linked to mining, are not adequately addressed in current regulations. Mongolia should establish comprehensive legal requirements for monitoring and addressing occupational diseases in the mining sector, ensuring that workers receive appropriate healthcare and compensation for work-related health conditions. By strengthening and expanding labor protections, the country can ensure safer, fairer working conditions for all mining workers while adhering to global standards.

The current legal framework for child labor falls short of international standards, particularly with respect to protecting children working in the informal sector or those who are self-employed. To align with international best practices, especially the ILO Conventions on Child Labor (No. 138 and No. 182), Mongolia should revise its Labor Code and related legislation to ensure comprehensive protection for all children, regardless of their employment status. It is recommended that the country expand the scope of child labor laws. The existing Labor Code, which sets the minimum age for formal employment at 16, should be expanded to include provisions that explicitly protect children in the informal sector and those who are self-employed. This would close the legal gap that leaves young workers unprotected, particularly in high-risk sectors such as mining and agriculture.

The government should introduce penalties for violating minimum age provisions. Mongolia's legal framework should impose clear and enforceable penalties for violations of the minimum working age. The absence of penalties for employing children under the age of 16 undermines the effectiveness of existing laws. Penalties should be imposed on any individual or entity that employs children below the legal age, with specific provisions for hazardous sectors like mining, where child labor poses severe health and safety risks.

Vulnerable groups, such as women and migrant workers, also require enhanced protections. The country's labor laws currently offer no tailored safeguards to address the unique challenges these groups face in mining operations. The government should introduce specific legal provisions that ensure fair treatment, safety, and support for these workers, aligning with international labor standards that protect all categories of workers. The country should also consider adopting gender-sensitive safety and health policies, such as specific guidelines for the provision of personal protective equipment tailored for women in mining.

Mongolia should adopt specific legal provisions to protect the rights of migrant workers in mining, ensuring they are not subject to exploitation, unsafe working conditions, or wage theft. These protections should align with international labor standards, such as the International Labour Organization Conventions on Migrant Workers. Migrant workers should be entitled to the same working conditions, pay, and safety standards as local workers.

In recent years, Resolution N. 296 and Resolution N. 355 have contributed to better regulation of artisanal and small-scale mining by formalizing operations and improving environmental standards. While these advancements reflect the country's commitment to aligning its mining practices with international standards, it should address gaps in gender-sensitive policies by integrating a gender perspective in Regulation N. 296 on the Extraction of Minerals by Artisanal and Small-Scale Mining. A comprehensive review of existing laws should be undertaken to include provisions that promote social protections for women in artisanal and small-scale mining, ensuring they are protected from gender-based violence, provided with safe working conditions, and included in economic opportunities.

Specific policies should be developed to establish social safety nets for women, especially those facing the dual burden of domestic and mining work. This would both enhance gender equality and create a more inclusive and secure mining environment in artisanal and small-scale mining, where women are particularly vulnerable.

To foster a cooperative and sustainable relationship between large-scale mining and artisanal and small-scale mining, the country should establish a clear regulatory framework that balances resource allocation, land use, and environmental protections. Resource allocation laws should define equitable access to mineral resources for both sectors to prevent conflicts. Land use planning should designate specific zones for large-scale mining and artisanal and small-scale mining, reducing land use disputes and ensuring that both sectors operate without interference. The government should enforce environmental regulations across both sectors to promote sustainable mining practices and responsible resource management. Additionally, recognizing community rights within mining laws and integrating conflict resolution mechanisms will empower local populations and promote peaceful relations in large-scale and artisanal and small-scale mining. Technical assistance programs in which large-scale mining companies support artisanal and small-scale mining with capacity-building initiatives to improve their health and safety practices should be encouraged. And partnerships should be developed that enable resource sharing and joint ventures for mutual benefit.

Governance Recommendations

Since joining the Extractive Industries Transparency Initiative in 2007, Mongolia has made progress in strengthening the governance of its mining sector, particularly by improving revenue transparency. The country has consistently published comprehensive reports on revenues from its mining and petroleum sectors, fostering greater accountability and public access to information. While these efforts have mitigated some governance risks, such as corruption and opaque resource management, further reforms are needed to close existing gaps in transparency, accountability, stakeholder engagement, and equitable revenue sharing in the sector.

To enhance transparency, the country should adopt policies that require public disclosure of mining tax revenues, including how these revenues are managed and distributed, in line with Extractive Industries Transparency Initiative standards. A recent study on contract transparency by the Natural Resource Governance Institute identified recommendations for Mongolia to revise the legal framework to mandate the disclosure of all relevant contracts and ensure consistent implementation.[56] It recommended improving SOE compliance with Mongolia's Glass Accounts Law (2014) which sets information disclosure requirements for government entities, including SOEs (footnote 56). Such transparency would not only allow for greater public scrutiny, but also mitigate the risk of corruption and ensure that mining companies are accountable for their tax contributions.

The country should establish mechanisms for stakeholder engagement and community consultation in the development and revision of policies that are designed to regulate the environmental and social impacts of the mining sector. Specific measures should be put in place to guarantee the inclusion of local communities, including seminomadic pastoralists, nomadic herders and ethnic minorities, in policy-related decision-making processes.

Civil society organizations suggested enhancing a number of measures to improve governance of the mining sector, including enhancing transparency in licensing and feasibility study approvals; revising legal frameworks to address overlaps and ensure enforcement of reclamation obligations; developing a vertical governance system for land management, linking national, municipal, and rural plans; establishing safeguards in the mine licensing process that include consultation and engagement with affected communities; and creating more independence between the mining sector (given the predominance of SOEs) and the monitoring of the mining sector.

In taxation and revenue sharing, Mongolia should develop policies that ensure equitable distribution of mining profits. Revenue-sharing frameworks should be established to ensure a portion of mining taxes is directed toward local development initiatives, such as infrastructure, healthcare, and education in mining-affected regions. This would create sustainable economic benefits and contribute to long-term development in these areas. Transparent and fair distribution of mining revenues nationally and locally is necessary for fostering inclusive economic growth in regions impacted by mining activities.

[56] Natural Resource Governance Institute. 2024. *Scoping Study on Contract Transparency in Mongolia*.

Finally, social investment initiatives should be incentivized or required through national legislation. Mongolia's tax laws should encourage mining companies to increase their social investment in the communities where they operate. Aligning these reforms with international frameworks such as the UN Guiding Principles on Business and Human Rights would ensure that mining companies contribute positively to the social and economic development of the regions they impact while adhering to sustainable and responsible business practices.

Incorporating these recommendations into the country's governance framework will improve transparency, accountability, and sustainability in the mining sector, benefiting local communities and the national economy.

8 | CONCLUSIONS

Mongolia's mining sector plays a vital role in the country's economic development, but ESG risks threaten its sustainability. Key environmental risks include weak biodiversity conservation, unsustainable water usage, and a lack of post-mining rehabilitation. Social risks are centered on inadequate labor protections, displacement of communities, and insufficient safeguards for vulnerable populations such as women and children. Governance gaps further exacerbate these challenges, with weak regulatory frameworks, limited transparency in revenue sharing, and poor stakeholder engagement.

To develop a climate-smart mining strategy, the country should prioritize sustainability in its extraction of critical minerals for the international renewable energy supply chain. This will require:

(i) **Strengthening environmental protections.** Mongolia should adopt stronger environmental regulations that enforce biodiversity conservation, sustainable water management, tailings management, and comprehensive mine closure plans. Mandatory emissions reduction targets, coupled with incentives for renewable energy integration in mining operations, will position the country as a leader in low-carbon mineral extraction.

(ii) **Enhancing social safeguards.** The government should mandate social impact assessments and ensure that labor laws align with international standards. Specific provisions should protect women and vulnerable groups, and community engagement and consultation should be made a legal requirement for mining projects throughout the mining life cycle. In some cases, where Indigenous Peoples are impacted, this may include the need to secure free, prior, and informed consent. Establishing benefit-sharing mechanisms and resettlement guidelines will help ensure that local communities see tangible benefits from mining operations.

(iii) **Improving governance and transparency.** Mongolia's mining sector will benefit from stronger governance mechanisms, including the robust enforcement of existing laws, the introduction of mandatory transparency measures, including requiring the disclosure of all relevant contracts, and the adoption of revenue-sharing frameworks. The government should establish mechanisms for stakeholder engagement and community consultation in the development and revision of policies that are designed to regulate the mining sector. By aligning these efforts with international best practices such as the Extractive Industries Transparency Initiative and Towards Sustainable Mining, Mongolia can enhance accountability and build trust between mining companies, the government, and local communities.

Civil society organizations also identified the need to strengthen the capacity of civil society to support communities in holding government and companies accountable to high ESG standards for mining; and suggested treating civil society organizations and affected communities as development partners, not just beneficiaries.

The future of Mongolia's mining sector lies in its ability to align with global sustainability standards while meeting the rising demand for critical minerals in the renewable energy sector. By integrating ESG principles into mining practices, the country can ensure the long-term viability of its mineral wealth, contribute to the global energy transition, and create shared value for its population. The development of a climate-smart, responsible mining strategy will not only mitigate environmental and social risks, but also position the country as a reliable supplier of critical minerals in the global marketplace, potentially fostering better cooperation with key international markets with increasingly stringent requirements around responsible sourcing of critical minerals.

REFERENCES

Action Research Report. 2014. *Mapping Gender-Based Violence and Mining Infrastructure in Mongolian Mining Communities*.

Asian Development Bank (ADB). 2020. *Making Water in Mongolia Available at the Right Time, at the Right Place, and in the Right Quality*. Brief No. 140.

ADB. 2020. Mongolia: *Labor Migration and Employment in the Mining Sector*.

ADB. 2020. *Vision 2050: Environment.*

ADB. 2024. *Country Climate and Development Report: Mongolia.*

ADB. 2024. *Towards Sustainable Mining Initiative Adoption in Mongolia.*

G. Batbayar et al. 2017. Chemical Water Quality Gradients in the Mongolian Sub-Catchments of the Selenga River Basin. *Journal of Environmental Monitoring and Assessment*. 189 (8).

Colorado State University. 2017. *Community-Based Rangeland Management in Mongolia: Outcomes and Keys to Success*. Mongolian Rangelands and Resilience (MOR2) Project.

B. Dalaibuyan. 2022. Negotiating the Coexistence of Mining and Pastoralism in Mongolia. *Journal of Contemporary East Asia Studies*. 11 (1). pp. 6–63.

Delve. 2023. *State of the Artisanal and Small-Scale Mining Sector Report*.

M. Dimovska. 2024. *Mongolia's Clean Energy Transition: Pathway to Sustainable and Inclusive Development*. United Nations Development Programme. 2 January.

U. Dovchin and S. Dovchin. 2024. The Discourse of the Anthropocene and Posthumanism: Mining-Induced Loss of Traditional Land and the Mongolian Nomadic Herders. *Journal of Ethnicities*. 24 (4).

Environmental Governance Programme (EGP). *Mongolia*. From the EGP for Sustainable Natural Resource Management (accessed 12 December 2024).

Environmental Impact Assessment Review. 2023. *Mongolian Mining Engagement with SIA and ESG Initiatives*.

Extractive Industries Transparency Initiative (EITI). 2023. *Mongolia Country Reports.*

J.D. Farrington. 2009. The Impact Of Mining activities on Mongolia's Protected Areas: A Status Report with Policy Recommendations. *Journal of Integrated Environmental Assessment and Management*. 2009. 1 (3). pp. 283–289.

Government of Mongolia. 2019. *Nationally Determined Contribution.*

Government of Mongolia. 2020. *Vision 2050: Economy*.

Intergovernmental Forum on Mining, Minerals, Metals and Sustainable Development (IGF). 2017. *IGF Mining Policy Framework Assessment: Mongolia*.

IGF. 2020. *Guidance for Governments: Improving Legal Frameworks For Environmental and Social Impact Assessment and Management*. International Institute for Sustainable Development.

IGF. 2023. *The Importance of Consultation and Engagement in Environmental and Social Impact Assessments*. IGF Case Study.

International Council on Mining and Metals (ICMM). 2019. *Handling and Resolving Local level Concerns and Grievances: Human Rights in the Mining and Metals Sector*. 10 December.

ICMM. 2021. *Position Statement: Climate Change*.

ICMM. 2024. *Position Statement: Nature*.

International Energy Agency. 2023. *Critical Minerals Market Review 2023*.

International Labour Organization. 2016. *Mongolia Briefing Note: Occupational Safety and Health in Mining*.

Land Portal. 2022. *Mining Fractures Land and Community in Mongolia*.

N. McIntyre et al. 2016. A Multi-Disciplinary Approach to Understanding the Impacts of Mines on Traditional Uses of Water in Northern Mongolia. *Journal of Science of the Total Environment*. 557–558. pp. 404–414.

Minority Rights Group. 2020. *Mongolia*.

Natural Resource Governance Institute (NRGI). 2023. *Diagnosing Corruption in the Extractives Sector: Mongolia Case Study*.

NRGI. 2024. *Scoping Study on Contract Transparency in Mongolia*.

NRGI. 2024. *Scoping Study on Extractive Sector State Owned Enterprise Disclosures in Mongolia*.

Open Government Partnership. 2019. *Mongolia: Improve Governance of State Owned Enterprises*.

Organisation for Economic Co-operation and Development (OECD). 2015. *Anti-Corruption Reforms in Mongolia*.

PwC. 2024. *Amendments to the Minerals Law and Related Tax Issues*.

E. Sodnomdarjaa et al. 2024. Resource Conundrum in Mongolia: Soil Contamination from Coal and Copper–Molybdenum Mining. *Journal of Soil Use and Management*. This reference quotes several studies.

T. Sternberg and A. Alhearn. 2023. Mongolian Mining Engagement with SIA and ESG Initiatives. *Journal of Environmental Impact Assessment Review*. 103.

The Nature Conservancy Mongolia Program. 2017. *Identifying Conservation Priorities in the Face of Future Development*.

Transparency International. n.d. *Country Profile: Mongolia*.

Transparency International. 2023. *Corruption Perceptions Index: Mongolia*.

Transparency International Mongolia. 2024. *Civil Society Report on the Implementation of the UN Convention Against Corruption in Mongolia*.

United Nations Development Programme (UNDP). 2022. *Business and Human Rights: National Baseline Assessment (Mongolia)*.

UNDP. 2024. *Gender Equality and Women's Empowerment in Leadership*.

UNDP Mongolia. 2019. *Training Manual on Responsible Mining*.

United Nations Economic Commission for Europe (UNECE). 2018. *Environmental Performance Reviews: Mongolia*.

UNESCO. 2024. *Mongol Nomad Migration and Its Associated Practices*.

United States Agency for International Development. 2021. *LandLinks. Mongolia Country Profile*.

United States Department of Labor. 2020. *Findings on the Worst Forms of Child Labor: Mongolia*.

US Department of Labor: Bureau of International Labor Affairs. 2023. *Child Labor and Forced Labor Reports: Mongolia*.

US Department of State. 2023. *2023 Country Reports on Human Rights Practices: Mongolia*.

University of Oxford. n.d. *Mitigating the Impact of Mining in Mongolia*. Oxford.

Wildlife Science and Conservation Center of Mongolia. 2014. *Biodiversity and Artisanal and Small-scale Mining in Mongolia*.

World Bank. 2020. *Mongolia's Mining Sector: Managing the Future*.

World Bank. 2024. *Mongolia Country Climate and Development Report: Overview*.

World Economic Forum. 2024. *Fostering Effective Energy Transition 2024*.

World Resources Institute. 2023. *Aqueduct Water Risk Atlas Country Rankings*.

World Wildlife Fund. 2020. *The Parliament of Mongolia has Approved 10 Areas for National Protected Areas*. 8 May.

Yale University and Columbia University. 2024. *Environmental Performance Index*.

www.ingramcontent.com/pod-product-compliance
Lightning Source LLC
Chambersburg PA
CBHW041800220926
51847CB00014B/269
9789292777227